'I wish someone had [...] so that I didn't was[...] know God.'

Peter Robinson, Professor of Computer Technology, University of Cambridge

'Read this book if you think that being an agnostic makes sense: or give it to anyone who says he/she does not know whether Christianity is true and whether it matters. The authors, with their idiosyncratic sense of humour, show that the big issues of life should not be ducked, and that to say "I don't know", for whatever reason, is a cop-out. Investigate the evidence, explore their reasoning and consider the most coherent explanation for the realities of life and death, and the impact of Jesus on those realities. I think you will find the book, short though it is, both challenging and compelling.'

Sir Jeremy Cooke, Retired High Court Judge

'So much more than a presentation of evidence, this book is a compelling argument for why sceptics should embrace asking questions of Jesus, and why the answers mean it's worth the effort. I enjoyed it all, and found myself strengthened in my own faith as I read. A gift for sceptics and believers alike – buy it and share it!'

Amy Wicks, Associate Pastor for Women's Discipleship, St Silas Church Glasgow

'A very intelligently written short book that explains with simplicity, humour and winsomeness the main tenants of the Christian faith. This will be edifying for believers and intriguing for agnostics. There is nothing quite like it in the market. I highly recommend this unique read.'

Gavin Peacock, Former Professional Footballer

'As I read this short book, to my surprise I found myself subconsciously making a list of family and friends I was desperately hoping would read it! Why was that? First because Sach and Gemmell have both taken very seriously and listened very hard to the questions of sceptics and agnostics. And secondly, because they have answered their questions with logic, learning and not a small dose of fun. I thoroughly recommend this eminently engaging and very useful book.'

Rico Tice, All Souls Langham Place and Christianity Explored

ARE YOU 100% SURE YOU WANT TO BE AN AGNOSTIC?

ANDREW SACH &
JONATHAN GEMMELL

10 Publishing
a division of 10 ofthose.com

British Library Cataloguing in Publication Data
A record for this book is available from the British Library

ISBN: 978-1-914966-34-7

Cover design by Simon Oliver
Typeset by Pete Barnsley (CreativeHoot.com)

Printed in Denmark by Nørhaven

10Publishing, a division of 10ofthose.com
Unit C, Tomlinson Road, Leyland, PR25 2DY, England

Email: info@10ofthose.com
Website: www.10ofthose.com

1 3 5 7 10 8 6 4 2

To Jacob Beynon
and to
Aileen and Isaac Gemmell

The Agnostic Diagnostic

Please take a few moments to complete the questionnaire over the page before you begin, rating each of the statements on the scale below.

1 Strongly agree	2 Agree	3 Neither agree nor disagree	4 Disagree	5 Strongly disagree
I regularly carry a placard around central London with this slogan.	I smile weakly at people carrying a placard with this slogan.	'Meh.'	I smile politely when someone expresses this opinion while inwardly despising them.	If someone expresses this opinion in my presence, I can't guarantee their safety.

☐ The Battle of Hastings took place in the year 1066.

☐ The universe created itself without any help from God (who doesn't exist).

☐ The teachings of Jesus and Muhammad are equally good for society.

☐ There is no such thing as absolute truth.

☐ Torture is absolutely wrong.

☐ Jesus defeated death and is alive today.

☐ More people should be vegans.

☐ My conclusions about Jesus are based on sufficient investigation.

☐ I'm 100% sure I want to be an agnostic.

In God We Doubt?

There's a joke doing the rounds at the moment that arguably isn't the best way to begin a book, because it doesn't work written down. But here goes anyway...

People in our society are becoming more religious. Most of them are nuns. When you ask them what religious beliefs they hold, they answer, 'Nun.' (Or actually they say, 'None,' which is why the joke only makes sense spoken out loud.) Ha ha ha.

Perhaps that's you, as you pick up this little paperback. You're a 'none'.

You're not a nihilist – theirs is the bleak philosophy that says there's no truth and no meaning and nothing matters. That's not you. You don't believe in *nothing* that much.

You're not an atheist – theirs is the belief (!) that there is no God, and everything we see came about purely by chance, and human beings are nothing but 'survival machines',[1] and human thoughts are no more than the movement of electrons and fluctuations in the concentration of neurotransmitters, and we are hurtling through space with no ultimate destiny besides the heat death of the universe. Personally, you're not that confident in God's non-existence.

You're not a fundamentalist. In fact you're quite concerned when people are committed to something so passionately that they are willing to die for it (and might, in some cases, kill others for it). Enthusiasts can be exclusive. Dogmatism is dangerous. Creeds can be cruel. Believers can be blinkered. Anything can be alphabetised. You are wary of the excesses of any belief system.

You prefer to identify as a humble agnostic. You're just not sure. You're not saying anyone is totally wrong, but neither are you prepared to say anyone has got it 100% right. In the Agnostic Diagnostic, you consistently scored somewhere in the middle. You want to be honest with yourself and with everyone else and hold up your hand and say, 'I just don't know.'

Agnosticism is on the rise. Wikipedia maintains a 'List of Agnostics', which includes the authors Franz Kafka and Matt Groening (of *Simpsons* fame); the tycoons Elon Musk and Warren Buffett; the actors Leonardo DiCaprio and Charlie Chaplin; the philosophers Noam Chomsky and David Hume; the scientists Marie Curie and Charles Darwin.[2] However, few have written explicitly in defence of their agnosticism. An exception is the broadcaster John Humphrys, who in 2008 published his book *In God We Doubt*:

> *So my own spiritual journey – if that's not too high-falutin' a notion – has taken me from my childish Big Questions to my ultimate failure to find any corresponding Big Answers. Along the way I have experienced the indoctrination of confirmation classes, the anticlimax of the Eucharist, the futility of prayer, the contradiction between the promises made by an allegedly merciful, loving God and the reality of a suffering world. So I end up – so far, at any rate – as a doubter.[3]*

Maybe you, like Humphrys, have had a religious upbringing or passed through a spiritual phase, but find that it no longer satisfies. Or perhaps you have always seen yourself as neutral. Possibly you'd quite like to believe in something out there, but you're not willing to commit unthinkingly. The comedian Marcus Brigstocke puts it well:

> *The truth, as I see it, is that I would rather stay in a place of confusion amongst similar restless souls shuffling about in the hope there might be a sign pointing in one direction or another, than leap aboard whichever bandwagon looks like it's got some momentum behind it and a confident driver. We might find God. We should probably have a plan for that in case we startle Him and He goes for us. I don't mind if we don't find Him. I'd be just as happy to discover that whatever road this is that I'm on, I'm not walking it alone.*[4]

Whatever your starting point, you're open-minded enough to have started a book that aims (we may as well be up front about this) to persuade you to abandon your agnosticism. Thanks. We want to reassure you at the outset that we are not into blind faith; we are into evidence, history, joy, forgiveness, truth, eternal life and honest self-reflection. We think some of what we have to share will surprise you. And we even dare to hope that by the end you won't be so sure that you are unsure.

I (Andrew) was once an agnostic myself, and this is the sort of book I wish someone had put into my hands as a confused teenager. I can sympathise with your questions, your indifference, your irritation, your fears. I'm pleased now to be a Christian and to have the opportunity to share how I got there.

I (Jon) have had many, many conversations with sceptics. This book contains the things, in hindsight, I wish I'd said.

In lieu of a contents page, here's an outline of the journey we hope you'll let us take you on. In 'What Kind of Agnostic Are You Anyway?' we discover that not all doubters are alike. In 'Meet the Truth', we consider the kind of evidence that convinced a bloke called John that his mate had created the universe. In 'Blind

Men Are Sometimes the Best Eyewitnesses!' we look in detail at one of Jesus' most famous miracles – and a first-century attempt to debunk it. In 'The Curious Case of Mr P', I (Andrew) talk about the time I was arrested, and we draw parallels between the British justice system and the weighing of biblical claims. In 'Even More Syllogisms (for the Enthusiast)', we apply ruthless logic to subjects like the Big Bang, the problem of suffering and the mystery of the Trinity. In 'It's Dangerous to Remain Agnostic', we explore why sitting on the fence is not in fact a neutral option. In 'Who's Playing Hide-and-Seek?' we turn the tables on the popular notion that God is elusive. In 'We Write This to Make Our Joy Complete', we tell the story of a phoney preacher whose faith, in the end, became authentic.

What Kind of Agnostic Are You Anyway?

The word *agnosticism* comes from the Ancient Greek *gnosis*, meaning 'knowledge'. The *a* at the start of the word just means 'not'. We say something is 'atypical' when it is not typical. Or 'asymmetrical' when it's not symmetrical. You could call a vegetarian an 'acarnivore' or someone who doesn't like bagpipes, 'aScottish'. If *gnosis* is about knowing, then agnosticism simply means not knowing.[5]

It is helpful to distinguish three types of agnosticism.

Type 1 is when something is knowable but you yourself don't know it. So, for example, I (Andrew) could say that 'I am agnostic about the neurological basis of ventriloquism – whether the brain mechanisms that determine a sound's

9

perceived location might be influenced by visual cues.' I used to know a bit about this when I did my doctorate in auditory neuroscience 20 years ago. I read a fascinating scientific paper on it, published in 1994. But I haven't kept up with the topic. Some scientists have probably taken the research further, and perhaps they now do know. I just haven't taken the time to read about their discoveries. So I'm agnostic.

In a similar vein, Jon is agnostic about how many helium balloons it would take for his wife Aileen to fly. It would be possible to know – a fairly simple experiment in fact – but because Aileen is afraid of heights, it didn't seem very kind to find out. So he's agnostic.

Perhaps you're agnostic about Jesus in this sense. It would be possible to know more about him, and some of your friends have come to firm conclusions, but you've not really looked into it sufficiently. And so you're agnostic.

Just as type 1 diabetes can be successfully treated with insulin injections, so we've found that type 1 agnosticism responds well to a course of historical research. If you're willing to take our advice as spiritual pharmacists, we'd recommend you read one of the first-century biographies of Jesus. Indeed, we'll be looking at one of them quite closely in later chapters.

Type 2 agnostics are shaking their heads at this point. For them, it's not just 'I don't know' but 'We *can't* know.' Theirs is a more entrenched philosophical conviction.

But wait a minute. There's an awkward irony here, because type 2 agnostics aren't very agnostic about their own position. To paraphrase, they are really saying, 'I *know* that you can't know.' Really? What makes them so sure that they can't be sure?

To declare, 'I know there is no compelling evidence for a God' is a bit like saying, 'I know there is no treasure hidden in Leicestershire.' How could you know this? You would have had to have first dug *everywhere*. What if there were a gold ingot deep beneath an inconspicuous cabbage field? Or a stolen diamond necklace inside a detergent bottle at a postcode the police did not check? It turns out the University of Leicester Archaeological Services – who, let's face it, do more digging than the rest of us – didn't even know until recently that

King Richard III was buried under their local car park.

(Some readers are wondering at this point about Heisenberg's uncertainty principle in quantum physics or Gödel's incompleteness theorem in Boolean algebra. If you know enough science to comprehend what these are, then you also know that they don't really apply to questions of history and God's existence. If the only Heisenberg you know is the badass antihero from a Netflix series about crystal meth, then you don't need to worry about it either.)

Type 2 agnosticism is tantamount to a claim to know *everything*. Only then could you be sure there wasn't some critical evidence that you'd missed. You'd need to know all history, to have bottomed out every philosophical question, to have explored every scientific avenue, including the ones we don't even know about yet. And you haven't! Unlike type 2 diabetes, which can often be managed by means of a careful diet, type 2 agnosticism puts people beyond help. It is both arrogant and irrational.

That just leaves the type 3 agnostic. For them, it's not 'I don't know' or 'I *can't* know' but 'I don't *want to* know, leave me alone.' Agnosticism is a defence against being cornered by a convert or pinned down by a preacher.

It reminds me (Andrew) of an unforgettable philosophy lecture by the late Dr Mike Ovey. He walked to the lectern with a twinkle in his eye and announced, mischievously, 'The world is flat. Convince me otherwise.' Then he folded his arms and waited.

'It looks round from space,' said someone. It was an inswinging yorker, heading straight for middle stump.

But Ovey just batted it away: 'NASA faked the photographs.'

'The magnetic field is ...' My fellow student Steve Jeffery, who already had a PhD in physics, came at him like a leg-spinner offering up a well-disguised googly.

'You're just trying to blind me with science,' said Ovey, leaving the ball well alone.

And so it went on. For 10 minutes, different bowlers did their best to bamboozle Mike 'Boycott' Ovey, but no one could catch him out. (Andrew apologises for not doing more to restrain Jon's cricket analogies.[6])

At that point an exasperated individual summed up the feeling of the room: 'It doesn't matter what arguments we make, you just find *any* reason to dismiss them, even if the reason is absurd!'

A broad grin spread across Ovey's face. 'Exactly. Today's lecture is on scepticism. Shall we make a start?'

Ovey then explained that the sceptics' quest (what we are calling type 3 agnosticism) is not to arrive at the truth, but rather to *avoid* arriving at the truth. They use agnosticism like a philosophical handbrake, to avoid being budged from the comfort of the status quo. They achieve this objective without even needing to raise their voices or engage in awkward confrontation. 'I don't know' suffices to ward off the most zealous Christian evangelist.

You'd think that sitting indefinitely on the proverbial fence would be uncomfortable, and it is, though with a bit of DIY and some memory foam it can be quite bearable. And it certainly seems preferable to the unknown and half-glimpsed horrors of what might lie on either side.

In the case of Christianity, agnosticism appeals not because of the fear that Christianity is not true, but because of the fear it's not *good*. There's a suspicion that God – if he's there – would want to spoil my life, limit my choices, suck out the fun. If Christianity had a colour, it would be grey. If you could sum up the Christian ethic in a word, it would be 'Don't'. Being a Christian means ill-advised fashion choices (socks and sandals), a wine cellar stocked only with Shloer[7] ('Christian champagne') and replacing your favourite Netflix thriller with back-to-back repeats of *Songs of Praise* on VHS.

Such is the caricature of Christianity that prevails in our post-Christian culture. It's why in 2008/9 the British Humanist Association raised over £150,000 to run an ad campaign on the side of buses proclaiming, 'There's probably no God. Now stop worrying and enjoy your life.' The implication was that the existence of God makes you anxious and miserable.

But what if that campaign was actually misinformation and fake news? What if a relationship with the God who made us is actually the key to security and joy?

A friend of ours was surprised to read in the Bible of Jesus turning water into wine. It wasn't the miracle that shocked him. Sure, $H_2O \rightarrow C_2H_5OH$ plus the subtle combination of tannins, catechins, flavonols and anthocyanins can't be done in a chemistry lab, but why shouldn't the God who made the universe do some party tricks? The surprise was that Jesus wasn't going around *turning wine into water*. Wasn't Jesus supposed to be anti-fun? And yet here he is creating the equivalent of more than 800 bottles of Châteauneuf-du-Pape to ensure that a party keeps going long into the small hours.

(The Bible is against *drunkenness*, and when you witness the tragic effects of alcoholism in a close friend's life, you realise that isn't actually fun at all. But if alcohol is enjoyed rightly, the Bible couldn't be more pro celebrations and friendship and viniculture).

What kind of agnostic are you anyway?

- Type 1: 'I don't know' – so it's time to find out.

- Type 2: 'I can't know' – don't be so absurd.

- Type 3: 'I don't want to know' – but maybe it's more wonderful than you imagined. Would you give it a hearing?

Meet the Truth

The White Cube gallery in Bermondsey recently hosted an exhibition of 350 paintings by Peter Dreher, the celebrated German artist. Each measured 10 by 8 inches. Each depicted the same empty glass of water. He has sketched the same glass almost daily since 1974.

A video of the painter at work, his brush painstakingly capturing every nuance of the refracted light, was utterly mesmerising. But almost more fascinating was the commentary associated with the project. We were informed that 'Dreher's studies of matter, light and time demonstrate that an artist's meditative focus can reveal great fulness, even in an empty glass,'[8] and that the work was 'as much a routine of coping and healing [Dreher lived through the aftermath of World War II] as it is an exploration of artistic conventions'.[9]

It's not unusual to find contemporary artists grappling with fundamental concepts about our existence. And they are not alone. The shelves of Waterstones are full of musings on what it means to be human, what it means to be male or female or non-binary, where we came from, where we are going, where we are now, the nature of consciousness, the nature of meaning, the nature of language and so on.

Philosophising is normal.

Andrew's stepbrother works for a concert hall in Essex. We just checked his Facebook and read that he's been for a pint at the Stag & Lantern, a micropub in Highams Park. Every day over a billion people log in to Facebook, and many of them upload descriptions of what they've been up to and who they've met.

Telling people what happened to you is normal.

It's normal to wrestle with the meaning of life. It's normal to record personal experiences. But these two types of 'literature' (if we can call them that) exist on different planes. You wouldn't say, 'Last night I met eternity in a micropub.' Or, 'You'll never guess who walked into the office on Monday afternoon – the beginning of the universe!'

That's really not normal. But it's exactly what a man called John wrote in a letter to some friends in Asia in the first century.

> *That which was from the beginning, which we have heard, which we have seen with our eyes, which we have looked at and our hands have touched – this we proclaim concerning the Word of life. The life appeared; we have seen it and testify to it, and we proclaim to you the eternal life, which was with the Father and has appeared to us. We proclaim to you what we have seen and heard, so that you also may have fellowship with us. And our fellowship is with the Father and with his Son, Jesus Christ.[10]*

John is talking about his encounter with Jesus of Nazareth, a carpenter's son, with whom he'd been on fishing trips, shared meals, travelled the length and breadth of Israel. He was convinced that Jesus was the manifestation of 'the eternal life', the one who existed 'from the beginning'. He was sure he had met God.

I (Jon) used to work in an office next to Andrew's. At no point in our employment together did I entertain the possibility that Andrew might be divine. On the contrary, I reached a firm conclusion about his non-divinity very early on. He performed no miracles. At times he failed to complete even simple tasks. It's a pretty clear-cut case.

Yet the apostle John somehow reaches the opposite verdict concerning Jesus. Not because of a vague dream he's had, or a zen-like trance he's fallen into after painting the same empty glass of water one too many times. Not because he's gullible or a few loaves short of a picnic. He is simply responding to what he and his friends have 'seen and heard' and 'our hands have touched'.

If you are tempted to tune out because you didn't see it with *your* eyes or touch it with *your* hands, park that thought. We'll come to the whole question of second-hand testimony soon. For now, we hope you're at least a little curious about how a first-century fisherman was persuaded that his mate had created the universe.

Perhaps he started to harbour suspicions at the wedding we've already mentioned, where Jesus turned water into wine. John describes this in the second chapter of his full-length biography of Jesus, known as John's Gospel. In chapter 4, he tells of a man who recovered from a life-threatening illness at exactly the moment that Jesus, a hundred miles away, pronounced him cured. 'But couldn't that just have been a coincidence?' asks the agnostic. Read on...

In chapter 5, John narrates Jesus' encounter with a man who had been a paraplegic for 38 years. Jesus tells him to 'pick up your mat and walk', and he does. This is a great one for those who are concerned that Jesus' miracles could be a set-up. It's one thing for a dishonest televangelist to slip someone a hundred quid to hobble up to the stage at a signs-and-wonders crusade and pretend to get 'healed'. It's another thing to suggest that Jesus, who at this point was about 33 years old, met this man five years before his own birth (!) and persuaded him to waste almost four decades feigning paralysis by a pool in the capital city in preparation for this encounter.

John reports that the healing took place 'in Jerusalem near the Sheep Gate [at] a pool, which in Aramaic is called Bethesda and which is surrounded by five covered colonnades'. For many years sceptics scoffed at this, because there was no other record of the pool's existence, nor any examples of pentagonal geometry in architecture of that time. The unorthodox French priest Alfred Loisy dismissed the five colonnades as a metaphor, with no basis in history. Then in 1956 an archaeological dig found the pool exactly as John described: not a pentagon, but a rectangle bounded by four colonnades, divided across the middle by a fifth.[11] *Oeuf sur le visage* for Monsieur Loisy!

In chapter 6, comes the feeding of the 5000, when Jesus was literally a few loaves short of a picnic. To be exact, the vast crowd had five bread rolls and two small fish to go round. The mental arithmetic is straightforward: there was 0.1% of a bread roll and 0.04% of a fish each, which makes it very surprising that after everyone had eaten their fill, John and his friends collected up 12 baskets of leftovers. Jesus had miraculously multiplied matter.

Shortly afterwards the disciples see Jesus waterskiing three or four miles offshore, with neither a boat nor waterskis. Walking on water is possible at the North Pole because the sea is frozen. It's gravitationally problematic on the Sea of Galilee in the Middle Eastern sun. But Jesus did it, and John saw it.

In chapter 9, Jesus heals a man born blind. We think that this miracle will be of particular interest to you, as an agnostic, and so we are going to devote the whole of the next chapter to it.

In chapter 11, Jesus arrives deliberately late for the funeral of his friend Lazarus. He is moved to tears as he joins the mourners, but moments later he raises Lazarus from the dead. 'What?' scoffs the sceptic. 'Can't you see this is just a legend, arising out of a perfect storm of overactive imaginations, scientific naivety and wishful thinking? They persuaded themselves that what they *wanted* to happen really *did* happen.'

But the details of John's narrative resist such easy dismissal. Sure, Lazarus' sisters believed in God, and they even believed Jesus had some kind of supernatural power. That's why they both reproached him on his arrival: 'if you had been here, my brother would not have died'. But they never expected a resurrection. Nor were they ignorant of the biochemistry of putrefaction. We discover this from their horrified reaction when Jesus asks them to open the tomb, rendered thus in a sixteenth-century English translation: 'Lord, by this time he stinketh, for he hath been dead four days!' In vain they urge Jesus not to go through with his macabre plan, but Jesus persists. They open the tomb. Jesus summons Lazarus. Lazarus emerges, looking like the mummy from a *Scooby-Doo* episode, still wrapped in strips of linen. Jesus instructs them to unwrap him. Jesus' enemies hurry to bury the evidence (pun intended).

In chapter 20, John records another resurrection that nobody expected. Roman soldiers had crucified Jesus two days previously just outside the city wall of Jerusalem, in front of a large crowd. John watched the whole thing. Victims of crucifixion, nailed through their hands and feet to a wooden cross, died in part from asphyxiation, as eventually they no longer had the strength to draw breath.[12] John records that, on this occasion, the Romans hastened death by breaking the legs of two criminals executed alongside Jesus (a practice known as *crurifragium*), but that this was unnecessary in Jesus' case, for he had already died. The executioners, being professionals, nonetheless verified his death by lancing his side with a spear, 'bringing a sudden flow of blood and water'.[13] Modern physiologists know that fluid accumulates in the pericardium and pleural cavity as a result of heart failure, which would explain this data. There could be no doubt that he was dead.

And none of the disciples expected to find him alive on Easter morning. Actually they *should* have expected it, for both Jesus and the ancient Jewish Scriptures had foretold his resurrection repeatedly.[14] But it's to the sceptic's advantage that they didn't, because it closes the door on the idea that they convinced themselves of an already held fantasy. Thus when Mary Magdalene discovers that the stone has been rolled away from Jesus' tomb, she doesn't jump to the conclusion that he has been raised, but simply reports, 'They have taken the Lord out of the tomb, and we don't know where they have put him!'

At this news, Peter and John run to the tomb. John is the faster runner (it is amusing that he, as author of the account, can't resist mentioning this) and when he arrives, spots Jesus' graveclothes lying there. Peter finally reaches the tomb, steps inside and notices that the fabric is arranged in a very particular way: with the linen that had covered the face separated from the linen that had covered the body. Why does this matter? If Jesus' body had been exhumed, the soldiers would surely have left the wrapping on the corpse. Even if, for some unexplained reason, they had removed the fabric, it would have been left in an untidy heap. But the graveclothes were left in exactly the same position as when Jesus had worn them, as if his body had passed right through. (John clearly intends both a comparison and a contrast with the raising of the mummified Lazarus.) When Peter shows John *this*, he believes.

Corpse

Grave Robber

Teenager

More evidence quickly follows as people start actually *meeting* the resurrected Jesus. Mary Magdalene encounters him in the garden near the tomb, initially mistaking him for the gardener. Later that evening a whole group of his disciples meet him in a locked room where they had remained in hiding, fearful that those who had called for Jesus' crucifixion would hunt them down too. This itself is significant, for only Jesus' resurrection can explain how a group of frightened followers were galvanised into the courageous martyrs whose message changed the world forever.

Finally, and most famously, Jesus appears to 'Doubting Thomas' (or, as we prefer to call him, 'Agnostic Thomas'). He is the patron saint of sceptics,[15] because he wasn't there when the others saw Jesus and he refused to accept their testimony: 'Unless I see the nail marks in his hands and put my finger where the nails were, and put my hand into his side, I will not believe.' The painter Caravaggio famously captured what happened next in his astonishingly lifelike painting *The Incredulity of Saint Thomas* (1601–1602), which we'd urge you to look up on Google

Images. At Jesus' invitation, Thomas performs the rather gruesome physical examination he demanded, and in doing so establishes at least three things:

- This is not a ghost, but a physical person (otherwise presumably Thomas' hand would have passed straight through).

- This person is alive.

- This is the same person that had been executed three days earlier (because Thomas examines the wounds of execution).

John alludes to this moment in the passage quoted earlier, when he writes of 'that ... which we have looked at and our hands have touched'. We might say that Thomas was not only an eyewitness but also a touch-witness.

Here's the question: Would it be reasonable, at this point, for Thomas to remain agnostic? Of course not. If he was actually there, and that is what he actually witnessed, then the only reasonable response is certainty. 'My Lord and my God!' he exclaims.

Blind Men Are Sometimes the Best Eyewitnesses!

24 November 2004 saw the results of the rigged Ukrainian presidential election broadcast live across the country on the state-run news network, UT1. The incumbent president, Viktor Yanukovych, had lost the vote but was about to announce that he had won. It was during this broadcast that sign language interpreter Nataliya Dmytruk shot to international fame: instead of announcing the victory of Viktor *Yanukovych,* Nataliya instead signed, 'Our president is Viktor *Yushchenko*. Do not trust the results of the central election committee. They are all lies.' Her courageous refusal to bend the truth to fit the official narrative eventually helped to spark the Orange Revolution, which saw a second vote and eventually a new government installed.[16]

In Ukraine, it was the deaf community who first discovered the truth that the governing authorities were keen to suppress. In chapter 9 of John's Gospel, it's a blind man. The parallels between him and Nataliya are surprisingly strong. We recommend that you read for yourself what is surely one of the most ironic and darkly comic chapters in the whole of the Bible. You can find it by searching for 'John 9' at www.biblegateway.com. The translation we are using in this book is the New International Version, though it doesn't matter much which you choose. (If you compare several, you'll discover the differences are minimal and the conspiracy theories about the Bible's message being lost in translation are spurious.)

Here's an A–Z synopsis of what happened:

a. Jesus meets 'a man blind from birth' on the road.

b. Jesus' disciples ask whether his blindness is God's punishment for a particular sin (akin to the notion of karma in Hinduism and other Eastern religions).

c. Jesus says that is not why the man is blind.

d. Jesus spits on the ground, makes some mud with the saliva, puts the mud on the man's eyes and tells him to wash in the Pool of Siloam (discovered by archaeologists in 2004).[17]

e. The man recovers his sight and goes home.

f. His neighbours are puzzled: 'Isn't this the same man who used to sit and beg?'

g. He tells them of his encounter with 'the man they call Jesus' and his miraculous mud.

h. They bring the man before the Pharisees (a group of ultraconservative Jewish leaders, who were considered experts in religious matters) and he repeats his testimony.

i. An argument breaks out about whether Jesus has broken God's law and so cannot be from God. The healing had taken place on the Sabbath (Saturday), and in the Ten Commandments, God had told the Jewish people, 'Remember the Sabbath day by keeping it holy…. On it you shall not do any work.'[18] Hence the controversy.

j. The Jewish leaders launch an investigation, and begin by interrogating the man's parents: 'Is this your son? … Is this the one you say was born blind? How is it that now he can see?'

k. The parents confirm their son's congenital blindness, but they are afraid to explain the healing because of sanctions already in place against followers of Jesus. Instead, they say their son can speak for himself: 'He is of age; ask him.'

l. So the man is brought again to the witness box for further questioning. The prosecution becomes hostile: 'Give glory to God by telling the truth … We know this man [Jesus] is a sinner.'

m. The man explains the key facts again: he was blind but can now see.

n. The Pharisees want to know how
    this happened.

o. The man asks why they need to hear the
    same details a second time: 'Do you want
    to become his disciples too?' he asks.

p. They start to hurl insults at him.

q. 'We are disciples of Moses!' they say
    (another allusion to their desire to
    uphold the Ten Commandments),
    'but as for this fellow, we don't even
    know where he comes from.' This
    is disingenuous, because a couple of
    chapters earlier they had complained
    that they *did* know where Jesus came
    from, and it wasn't mysterious enough
    for them: 'When the Messiah comes, no
    one will know where he is from'.[19]

r. The man repeats the key facts a third
    time: 'He opened my eyes.' He offers
    his own logical deduction from the
    evidence and challenges theirs (more on
    this below).

s. They turn nasty and accuse him of
    being 'steeped in sin at birth' (the same

karma-like view of disability that Jesus had earlier disavowed). They throw him out.

t. Jesus catches up with the man and asks him whether he believes in the 'Son of Man' (a Messianic title from the Jewish Scriptures). 'Who is he, sir? … Tell me so that I may believe in him.'

u. Jesus replies, 'You have now *seen* [!] him; in fact, he is the one speaking with you.'

v. The man worships Jesus.

w. In a gripping final scene Jesus turns the whole court case upside down. Previously he was the accused. Now he arrives as the Judge.

x. 'For judgment I have come into this world, so that the blind will see and those who see will become blind,' says Jesus.

y. The Pharisees ask whether, by this enigmatic statement, he is implying that they are blind.

z. You betcha.

This is an account of someone who moves from blindness to sight, but also from agnosticism to faith. At the beginning he refers to Jesus simply as a 'man'. Halfway through the episode he calls Jesus a 'prophet'. By the end he is worshipping him as God. Ironically it is the Pharisees' hostile cross-examination that causes him to make progress in his own thinking: 'Whether [Jesus] is a sinner or not, I don't know. One thing I do know. I was blind but now I see!'

From what is certain (the healing), he then starts to draw logical conclusions about who Jesus must be. The same can't be said for the Pharisees. To help us evaluate their juridical process, we consulted London barrister Ed Crossley. He made three points.

First, the *ad hoc* trial is conducted *in absentia*. (Thanks, Ed. *Omnes optimi advocati lingua Latina utuntur.*)[20] Jesus is the one on trial, but he is not present in the courtroom; his evidence isn't heard, and he's given no opportunity to defend himself.

Second, the Pharisees are biased: 'We *know* this man [that is, Jesus] is a sinner,' they say. Ed would like to ask them, in cross-examination, exactly how they know this? Isn't that the question the trial is supposed to answer? Yet they have already decided the verdict and pay no attention to the testimony given.

Third, the Pharisees manipulate the evidence. They engage in witness intimidation (this is the reason the blind man's parents refuse to testify in detail), they ask leading questions and they bully the witness.

Scholars of logic evaluate arguments by expressing them in syllogisms, where premises are distinguished from conclusions that are supposed to follow from them. Let's now use that tool to compare the reasoning of the Pharisees and the (formerly) blind man:

Pharisees	Man born blind
Premise 1: Jesus is a sinner.	*Premise 1:* I was healed.
Premise 2: God doesn't listen to sinners.	*Premise 2:* God doesn't listen to sinners.
Conclusion: You weren't healed.	*Conclusion:* Jesus is not a sinner.

In the Pharisees' case, the presupposition 'Jesus is a sinner' trumps the evidence of the healing –

and so they conclude that he wasn't healed after all. In the man's case, the actual evidence of the healing trumps the presupposition – and so he concludes that Jesus isn't a sinner after all.

We have a name for the blind man's methodology. It's called science. Whereas the Pharisees' approach of ignoring observed data because of an unbudging commitment to an existing theory hasn't generally helped the progress of science:

Popular view	Copernicus' view
Premise 1: The sun orbits the earth.	*Premise 1:* My observations show the earth orbits the sun.
Premise 2: Copernicus' observations suggest the earth orbits the sun.	*Premise 2:* Your theory says that the sun orbits the earth.
Conclusion: Copernicus' experiments are wrong.	*Conclusion:* Your theory is wrong.

Of course, some people use science to deny the possibility of miracles, but again it helps to set out two types of reasoning side by side:

Popular view	**Alternative view**
Premise 1: Miracles are impossible.	*Premise 1:* Jesus did miracles.
Premise 2: The Bible claims Jesus did miracles.	*Premise 2:* Atheists deny the existence of a divine being such as could do miracles.
Conclusion: The Bible is wrong.	*Conclusion:* Atheists are wrong.

What are your premises? Are the premises valid? Are they based on evidence or on your own presuppositions? What are your conclusions? Do they logically follow?

Ruthless logic cured the blind man of his agnosticism. Perhaps it will for you too. For those who are particularly enjoying these syllogisms, we've included a few more in a later chapter.

But the Pharisees are obstinate sceptics. They are impervious to the evidence. They are, to pick up on Jesus' verdict on them, *blind*. There is no physical problem with their vision, but there is a spiritual problem with their hearts.

According to Jesus, we all share this disability. Our agnosticism is the sign of a deep internal blindness that we need God's help to overcome. We will return to that in a later chapter.

For now, let's return to the parallel with Nataliya Dmytruk. Despite the adverse political climate, she had the courage to testify to the truth. And so did the formerly blind man. Persecution of Christians was rife in the first century, but he was one of many who nevertheless spoke up for what he had seen. Blind men are sometimes the best eyewitnesses.

The Curious Case of Mr P

On 12 May 2013, I (Andrew) was arrested. Having left church on my bicycle less than half an hour earlier, I found myself in the back of a police car, under caution, on suspicion of committing assault.

By the time we got to the police station, another version of the facts had emerged, and I was allowed to go. Meanwhile, my accuser was arrested for assaulting *me*, and was later convicted in court. None of the three magistrates saw what happened, but they reached a guilty verdict on the basis of the testimony of two eyewitnesses.

Here's what happened. An elderly couple from our church had taken their time reversing out of a tight parking space, and temporarily blocked a white van that was delivering a crane part to the construction site of a now famous London skyscraper. The van driver, who I now know as Mr P, became impatient, revved his engine and mounted the curb to push past, reaching his destination only a few yards further on. I challenged him about his aggressive driving but he told me to f*** off, and I cycled away.

Mr P followed me in his van and, in a quiet street round the corner, overtook me and swerved left to block my path. He then got out of the van, pushed me to the floor and was about to beat me up. A security guard intervened. He had been seated in the vast atrium of a large, glass-fronted office building, looking out onto the street with an unbroken view of the action. The police were called. When they arrived and asked what happened, I said, 'He assaulted me.' Quick as a flash, Mr P replied, 'No, *he* assaulted *me*.' And so they arrested us both pending their investigation.

Some people sniff at eyewitness evidence when it comes to Jesus. 'I would have to have seen it for myself,' they say. But the fact is we live in a country where eyewitness testimony is enough to put you in prison (or have you released from police custody).

Of course, witnesses can lie. They can be mistaken. They can forget. But that doesn't mean that human testimony is worthless. You just need carefully to evaluate it, as the courts routinely do. We spent the last chapter looking at how the Pharisees handled evidence corruptly. Let's now think about the criteria for a fair legal process.

For example, did it matter that one of the bystanders called to testify against Mr P was a member of the church I attended? Not necessarily – sympathy is not the same as bias. When someone complains that you shouldn't trust reports about Jesus written by Christians, we sometimes cheekily reply that you shouldn't trust books about medicine written by doctors. Obviously doctors believe in medicine, just as Christians believe in Jesus, just as my friends believed in my innocence. But that doesn't mean they fabricated their reasons for doing so.

A key question for the magistrates would be whether the witnesses were in a position to benefit from their testimony. For example, if it were discovered that I had made a large deposit into a Swiss bank account in my friend's name, his words would be discredited. But the early Christians didn't get rich for writing the gospels. The grim picture of corrupt bishops living in luxurious palaces at the expense of downtrodden peasants (as if Jesus had never warned that the love of money is the root of all evil) was centuries away. The first Christians were marginalised, persecuted, rejected, even martyred. They gained nothing in this world, save for the relationship with God that Jesus promised, and the hope of life beyond the grave.

There's a simple logic at work here:

1. You won't die for a lie *you know is a lie*. The words in italics are important. Those who decided to fly a Boeing 767 into a Manhattan skyscraper really believed that it would be their passport to a virgin-filled paradise. But had they known this was false, they would never have turned up at the airport.

2. You may not be prepared to die for something even if you know it's true. Life is precious and few causes are worth giving everything for. There aren't many Emily Wilding Davisons among us.

3. You *would* be willing to die for someone who could save you from death. I mean,

if you were really sure he could – if the person who said he could save you from death was himself saved from death, and you saw him alive after his death, and your friend Thomas stuck his fingers in the wound made by the executioner while you looked on. Then it would make a lot of sense to give your life for him. And that's what his disciples did.

Let's now consider the proximity of witnesses to the events. Would it have mattered if instead of the security guard himself testifying against Mr P, he had told his cousin, who told her dental hygienist, who told her tennis partner, and she was the one appearing in court? Yes, that would matter! No one wants to base a legal decision on fourth-hand evidence.

Many assume that the evidence of the Bible is fourth- or fifth- or tenth- or twentieth-hand, and so wonder whether Jesus' divinity might be the outcome of a game of Chinese Whispers gone horribly wrong.[21] But we've already seen that John, one of the biblical authors, was actually there. Matthew, similarly, was one of

Jesus' twelve apostles, while Mark and Luke were close associates of the early disciples. Nor is it plausible that their messages were changed as they were passed on, because of some key differences between children at a birthday party and Christian scribes:

Chinese Whispers	Transmission of biblical manuscripts
The children pass on the message by whispering, amid a cacophony of giggles, gossiping parents and the sound of Uncle Clive cueing up the music for pass the parcel.	One scribe reads aloud from the manuscript as other scribes meticulously make their copies. They can then check their work against the original.
Each child whispers to one other child, so the message passes along a line.	The same manuscript is copied many times so that the message branches out like a tree.
At the end of the game we listen only to the child at the end of the line, where the message has become maximally corrupted.	Scholars collect multiple manuscripts from different continents and centuries, sampling many points of the copying process. They then carefully compare all of them.

The fact that manuscripts were duplicated and distributed far and wide has this consequence: any mistake (or deliberate change) made later than the original becomes glaringly obvious. Imagine a rogue scribe in Alexandria in the fifth century decides to alter Jesus' mother's name to Amy. Others faithfully copy him so that there arises a whole Alexandrian manuscript tradition that speaks of the Virgin Amy. Meanwhile, scribes outside Alexandria and all manuscripts before the fifth century call her Mary. A modern scholar, with the documents side by side, would spot the scribal mischief at once. In fact there are remarkably few discrepancies between copies of the New Testament collected from across the world and across the ages; the important ones are footnoted in modern Bibles (so there's no attempt to cover them up), and none calls into question a major tenet of the Christian faith.

Let's now turn to the question of suppressed counterevidence. Would it matter if there were other witnesses whose testimony supported Mr P who were never called to the stand? Yes, that would matter very much. Dan Brown's bestseller

The Da Vinci Code popularised the conspiracy theory that the fourth-century Roman Emperor Constantine censored various alternative gospels in favour of the four whose version of Jesus he happened to prefer.[22] Matthew, Mark, Luke and John have come to be more 'official' but aren't necessarily more historical, he suggests.

There are a number of reasons why this is nonsense. First, there is evidence that the early church (long before Constantine) knew of only four gospels. The second-century bishop Irenaeus famously wrote:

> *It is not possible that the Gospels can be either more or fewer in number than they are. For, since there are four zones of the world in which we live, and four principal winds ... it is fitting that [the Church] should have four pillars.... He who was manifested to men, has given us the Gospel under four aspects.[23]*

When the second-century writer Tatian wanted to compile material from all of the gospels into a single narrative, known as the Diatessaron, he used only the traditional four. The Muratorian

Fragment, thought to be the earliest list of New Testament books, refers only to the traditional four. And so on.

Second, the alternative gospels – such as Thomas, Philip, or Mary – are demonstrably fakes. They date from the mid-second century onwards and so by definition contain no useful eyewitness material. They mention hardly any place names, because their authors had never been to Israel. In the passage about paying taxes to Caesar, Thomas drops a clanger by mentioning a gold coin, whereas Mark correctly refers to the denarius (made of silver). Theologically, they are out of step with the rest of the New Testament, being preoccupied with the need for the soul to escape the physical body – this was a popular Greek idea that Paul explicitly refutes in 1 Corinthians.

Third, Dan Brown's specific suggestion that the biblical gospels are anti-women, and that the Gnostic gospels restore the balance, shows he has read neither! Some of the greatest heroes in Mark's Gospel are women – the Syro-Phoenician, the widow in the temple, the woman who anoints Jesus. Conversely, it's hard to find a more misogynistic statement than that which closes the Gospel of Thomas:

> Simon Peter said to Him, 'Let Mary leave us, for women are not worthy of Life.' Jesus said, 'I myself shall lead her in order to make her male, so that she too may become a living spirit resembling you males. For every woman who will make herself male will enter the Kingdom of Heaven.'[24]

Oh dear!

Let's move on to one of the thorniest issues of all: does it matter that the testimonies against Mr P differed slightly from each other? Irreconcilable contradictions between witness statements are a sure sign that someone is lying. On the other hand, small discrepancies are the very hallmark of authenticity. Two people reporting on the same event will each remember different details, from different perspectives, that may at first sight appear to be in tension. 'Mr P drove off very fast' and 'Mr P drove slowly' are both valid recollections of a scenario in which Mr P sped past Witness A but then braked before turning slowly into the side road beside Witness B. When it comes to the gospel accounts, atheist bloggers are quick to cite supposed contradictions without giving them careful thought. A classic is the suicide of Judas Iscariot, the disciple who betrayed Jesus for money. In the biblical book of Acts, we are told that he bought a field with the proceeds and 'there he fell headlong, his body burst open and all his intestines spilled out'. But in Matthew's Gospel, we are told that, full of remorse, he tried to return the blood money and hanged himself; the chief priests then used the money to buy the 'Field of Blood'.[25] How did he die? Who bought the field?

Notice first of all how much overlap there is. Both accounts agree that this field was purchased with money given in exchange for betraying Jesus. Both accounts agree that Judas died violently there. From a historian's perspective, it's a plus that these central facts emerge from superficially dissimilar accounts, because it's unlikely that the authors have colluded.

Neither are the differences irreconcilable. What if Judas hanged himself (Matthew) and the rope subsequently broke such that he fell and burst open (Acts)? What if saying that Judas bought the field (Matthew) is a shorthand for the chief priests buying it in his name and with his money (Acts)? You may not agree with this way of reconciling them,[26] but to dismiss two historical sources wholesale on account of minute divergencies in their narration of a single episode is an approach that, taken to the British courts, would destroy the justice system!

Finally, does it matter that Mr P did not have any forensic evidence against him? There was no 'science' – DNA matches, tyre skid mark analysis, ballistic reports (thankfully!) – only the words of those who were there. I (Andrew) remember attending a dinner at which the ultra-sceptical Oxford professor Peter Atkins urged us not to believe anything except what could be proved by scientific experiment. It sounds sensible, until you realise that … somewhat ironically his advice itself cannot be proved by scientific experiment. Nor was it possible, by his criterion, to verify that he even gave the advice. Sure, there were 300 or so eyewitnesses who had heard him minutes before and could testify to the fact, but his words left no trace that could be recovered in a laboratory.

Here's the point: science is powerful, but it would be foolish to suggest it's the only kind of evidence we need. Jon can't prove 'scientifically' that he was born on 26 October, or that his wife loves him, or that he saw a man dressed as an elf riding a Boris bike along Borough High Street last December, though each of these facts can be confirmed by individuals in a position to know (Jon's mum, Jon's wife and the fellow commuters who gazed at Santa's little helper with similar surprise).

In this chapter, we have touched on a few of the reasons why we consider the biblical testimony to Jesus reliable. Some of you are thinking, 'They haven't convinced me; I'm still not sure.' And that's OK, but what are you going to do with this agnosticism? If you're honest about wanting to reach the truth, you mustn't let it go. There's more you can read – for a start, we would recommend *Can We Trust the Gospels?* by Cambridge scholar Peter Williams, an academically rigorous yet wonderfully accessible book.[27] Even better, get hold of a New Testament and start to read it for yourself.

Don't wallow in your agnosticism! Start investigating!

Even More Syllogisms (for the Enthusiast)

If you enjoyed the syllogisms in 'Blind Men Are Sometimes the Best Eyewitnesses!' you might want to ponder a few more. If you've had enough of them, feel free to skip to the next chapter.

On the creation of the world

People once thought that the universe was eternal. Now it's almost universally agreed that the universe had a beginning in the finite past – both the Bible and the Big Bang theory say so. But that gives atheists a headache:

Atheist view	The Kalam cosmological argument[28]
Premise 1: There is nothing beyond the physical universe.	*Premise 1:* Things don't 'just happen' without a cause.
Premise 2: The physical universe went from non-existence to existence (the Big Bang).	*Premise 2:* The physical universe went from non-existence to existence.
Conclusion: The universe 'just happened' with no cause beyond itself.	*Conclusion:* The physical universe had a cause beyond itself, namely God.

'But who created God then?' comes the atheist's reply. Nobody did. He is eternal, with no beginning in time. He has never *not* existed (in this respect he is different to the universe) and so he didn't need anyone to cause him.

There's a lot more to say about God's creation of the world. It explains our intuition that we are more than just atoms; that the personal can't be reduced to the impersonal; that joy and love and beauty (and, for that matter, grief and hate and ugliness) can't be explained adequately in terms of neurobiology alone; that moral decisions are ultimately answerable to an unchanging external standard, such that evil remains evil even when a particular society evolves to accept it as normal.[29] All of this makes sense if humans are made in the image of God, who is loving and personal and good, and who will one day judge the world in righteousness.[30]

Atheist view	Christian view
Premise 1: Human life can be reduced to material causes.	*Premise 1:* Good and evil are fundamental concepts.
Premise 2: Material causes are indifferent to good and evil.	*Premise 2:* Material causes are indifferent to good and evil.
Conclusion: 'Good' and 'evil' are arbitrary labels with no ultimate basis.	*Conclusion:* Human life cannot be reduced to material causes.

The idea that we are the product of a Divine Mind accounts also for why the universe seems 'finely tuned', as though its many parameters have been deliberately chosen so as to make life possible. The physicists tell us, for example, that if the ratio of the electromagnetic force constant to the gravitational force constant were increased or decreased by 1 part in 10^{40}, then we would have a universe containing either only big stars (too hot to sustain life) or only small stars (too cold to manufacture chemical elements). Or that if the ratio of the expansion and contraction forces acting just after the Big Bang had altered by as little as 1 part in 1055, then the universe would either have expanded too quickly so that no galaxies formed, or too slowly so that it quickly collapsed. John Lennox, Emeritus Professor of Mathematics at Oxford University, discusses these examples and others in his book *God's Undertaker: Has Science Buried God?*, which we'd highly recommend to anyone who is sceptical on scientific grounds.[31]

On the problem of suffering

The enormity of human suffering is too serious a matter to be trivialised with a syllogism. Better to start by showing real compassion, as Jesus himself did. Better to seek to alleviate pain and poverty, as his followers have done throughout history, founding hospitals, providing education, campaigning against slavery, seeking justice.[32] Better to show how the biblical worldview of a 'paradise lost' – God's once flawless creation now corrupted by our sin – uniquely explains our sense that the world *ought* to be better than it *is*; and explains the resulting mixture of fulfilment and regret, gladness and guilt that characterises our lives. Better to share the Christian hope of a new creation where God 'will wipe every tear from their eyes' and where 'There will be no more death or mourning or crying or pain, for the old order of things has passed away.'[33] Better to point to the Christ who himself willingly suffered on the cross to win that glorious future for his people. Better to pause in wonder at his extraordinary grace and humility, and to pray with a World War I poet:

The other gods were strong; but Thou wast weak;
They rode, but Thou didst stumble to a throne;
But to our wounds only God's wounds can speak,
And not a god has wounds, but Thou alone.[34]

Yet, not infrequently, some smug philosopher trots out the facile argument below, to which we reply, once again, by simply reversing a couple of the terms:

Atheist view	Christian view
Premise 1: There are no circumstances in which a loving God would allow suffering.	*Premise 1:* A loving God exists.
Premise 2: Suffering exists.	*Premise 2:* Suffering exists.
Conclusion: A loving God does not exist.	*Conclusion:* There are some circumstances in which a loving God would allow suffering.

What reasons could God possibly have for allowing suffering though? No doubt there are many, some of which we may not understand. But Jesus gives the starkest one: suffering is a wake-up call, a warning shot, a sign that something is terribly wrong. We need to turn to God before it's too late.[35]

On the mystery of the Trinity

Usually it's the atheist who assumes he has the logical upper hand when debating Christians, and so our syllogistic sword fight has so far been with him. But we turn now to parry an attack brought by the Muslim and the Jehovah's Witness:

Islamic / Jehovah's Witness view	Christian view
Premise 1: God is a singular entity.	*Premise 1:* Jesus is God.
Premise 2: Jesus was sent by God, from whom he is distinct.	*Premise 2:* Jesus was sent by God the Father, from whom he is distinct.
Conclusion: Jesus can't be God	*Conclusion:* God is not a singular entity, but exists as a loving union of three persons: Father, Son and Holy Spirit.

At which point the sceptic objects that the doctrine of the Trinity is just too mysterious to be believable, leading us to another pair of syllogisms:

Sceptical view	Christian view
Premise 1: I ought to be able to understand everything about God.	*Premise 1:* The doctrine of the Trinity is true.
Premise 2: I don't fully understand the doctrine of the Trinity.	*Premise 2:* I don't fully understand the doctrine of the Trinity.
Conclusion: The doctrine of the Trinity must be false.	*Conclusion:* I do not understand everything about God.

It's perfectly reasonable to expect that finite creatures would not be able fully to comprehend an infinite Diving Being. The mould growing on your strawberry jam doesn't understand the command 'Sit!' Andrew's cocker spaniel Gustave does (sometimes) understand the command 'Sit!', but he doesn't understand quantum mechanics. I (Andrew) did once understand a bit of quantum mechanics, but I don't fully understand the Trinity. Sure, I'm more intelligent than Gustave, and he's marginally more intelligent than a fungus. But what makes me think that the human mind is the *ultimate* measure of truth? Couldn't there be someone higher up the chain than me?

On the relevance of Jesus to you

We thought we'd close with a provocative one:

Sceptical view	**Christian view**
Premise 1: There's nothing in my life that I need fundamentally to change.	*Premise 1:* As the Son of God, Jesus is relevant to me.
Premise 2: Jesus called people to 'repent' – that is, fundamentally to change.	*Premise 2:* Jesus called people to 'repent' – that is, fundamentally to change.
Conclusion: Jesus is irrelevant to me.	*Conclusion:* There must be things in my life that I need fundamentally to change.

It's Dangerous to Remain Agnostic

King's bishop to b5. The Ruy Lopez. You've researched the opening 10 moves deep, and as the game progresses you become hopeful of a checkmate.

You're so focussed on the board that you are unaware of whatever else is happening around you. Rook to d7, check. Your opponent resigns. You shift back your chair. You can see only the board. Everything else is a blur.

Reaching to shake your opponent's hand, you see his outstretched palm, but his elbow disappears into the fog. His face is hidden. 'I really need an early night,' you think. 'A full day's work and a chess game is a bit too much at my age.'

On the drive home, your peripheral vision is back to normal, but when you get back to your house, you drop your keys and you spend ages hunting around for them. The next morning you can see the muesli, but the bottle of semi-skimmed has vanished completely from view, though it turns out to be only inches away.

You text your boss. You queue for an emergency GP appointment. She makes an urgent referral. Next thing you know, you're trying to keep still as your body is slowly enveloped by the buzzing tunnel of the MRI machine. As you emerge, the radiographer's face is inscrutable.

'It's a pituitary gland tumour,' says Dr Owusu, the consultant oncologist, later that afternoon. 'I recommend endoscopic transnasal transsphenoidal surgery. In plain English, that means we put a tiny tube up your nose and cut away the tumour. Then a course of radiotherapy. If we act immediately, you should make a full recovery.'

On the bus home, you realise you can see out of the corner of your eye without any difficulty. Specifically, you can read the title of the book your fellow passenger is reading: *The Health Conspiracy: How Doctors, the Drug Industry and the Government Undermine Our Health*. The next day you feel great. In your lunch hour you win two games consecutively on lichess.org and your rating goes up to 1424. You ask your colleague, 'How do I look? I've been feeling a bit under the weather recently.'

'You look fine,' she says.

You don't know if you can trust Dr Owusu and you're having doubts about his diagnosis – not least because the prospect of his colleagues deploying a robotic knife up your right nostril is singularly unappealing. It's time for a second opinion.

At the Greenwich Alternative and Holistic Medicine Centre, you meet Ms Foxglove. To the accompaniment of a soothing soundtrack of porpoise calls, she reassures you that everything is OK, though a course of echinacea could help unblock your sinuses.

Echinacea by mouth to clear the nose. Or a robot up the nose to clear the head. Which to choose?

A month later you have missed your follow-up appointment with Dr Owusu because of the traffic, and you haven't rescheduled yet because it's a busy time with the end of the tax year, but you promise yourself that you will. The headaches are bad sometimes. But not always. Holland & Barrett are doing two for one on echinacea.

You've probably realised by now that this is a parable about the dangers of agnosticism. To remain undecided about medical matters can be fatal.

There are three apparent options:

1. Put your faith completely in Dr Owusu. Face the surgery. Endure the subsequent radiotherapy.

2. Reject Dr Owusu as a medical fraud. Dismiss the headaches and enjoy life.

3. Be agnostic. Delay hospital appointments. Reserve judgement.

In fact options two and three are functionally the same. Failing to decide means the decision is made for you.

Is this a fair analogy though? We could tell another story in which the topic you're agnostic about is the best flavour of gelato. And who cares if, while you're sitting on the fence and ruminating about the benefits of fragola versus stracciatella, the ice-cream shop closes and you go without – it's probably better for your waistline anyway. Not all indecision is life-threatening. The question is this: Is the Bible's message more like an ice-cream flavour or a medical emergency?

The apostle John's first letter, the opening paragraph of which we looked at earlier, goes on to summarise the Christian message in just eleven words: 'God is light; in him there is no darkness at all.'[36]

It means God is good, and there is no evil in him. It means God is true, and there is no falsehood in him. But all of us are a mixture of good and bad, of integrity and lies.

I (Andrew) used to brush my teeth to the dim glow of one of the original energy-saving lightbulbs. It saved energy chiefly by emitting almost no light. I looked fantastic. I could never understand why rich celebrities would fill their bathroom ceilings with thousands of lumens worth of recessed LEDs. Who wants to be confronted daily with the harsh reality of a nose densely populated with blackheads and coffee-yellowed teeth?

In the dark, most of us look OK (though some of you look sinister, to be frank). But in the light of God's blazing purity, we have only two options:

If we claim to have fellowship with him and yet walk in the darkness, we lie and do not live out the truth. But if we walk in the light, as he is in the light, we have fellowship with one another, and the blood of Jesus, his Son, purifies us from all sin.[37]

In other words, you can *claim* to be God's friend while being shady. Churches (and mosques and temples and even secular charities' fundraising dinners) are full of people playing 'let's pretend', who hope that the veneer of religion or respectability will compensate for a chequered past. But it's all a fake. The alternative, according to John, is to turn back to God and start living his way; in doing so, we discover the cleansing that Jesus bought for us by his death on the cross.

A quick aside here, because John doesn't quite say what many Christians expect. They rightly emphasise that God's grace is for free and isn't earned by our moral endeavour. But pushed too far, that can sound as though Christian ethics are an optional extra for the enthusiast. Surprisingly, John urges us that we must step into the light *first*. Surely he took his inspiration from the Lord Jesus himself, who challenged his hearers, 'Anyone who chooses to do the will of God will find out whether my teaching comes from God or whether I speak on my own.'[38] You have to try it to know that it's real. Our friend Rico Tice likens it to a sliding door in front of a department store – you have to step towards it before it will open.

John continues:

> *If we claim to be without sin, we deceive ourselves and the truth is not in us. If we confess our sins, he is faithful and just and will forgive us our sins and purify us from all unrighteousness.*[39]

In other words, it's possible to lie successfully even to yourself: 'I'm a great guy, really I am.'

But psychiatrists tell us that buried guilt and repressed consciences are a ticking time bomb. The alternative, according to John, is to 'come clean' in order for Jesus to clean you. A clear conscience is an indescribable blessing.[40]

John further continues:

> If we claim we have not sinned, we make him out to be a liar and his word is not in us. My dear children, I write this to you so that you will not sin. But if anybody does sin, we have an advocate with the Father – Jesus Christ, the Righteous One. He is the atoning sacrifice for our sins, and not only for ours but also for the sins of the whole world.[41]

In summary, to deny there's a problem is to lie to each other, to lie to ourselves and – worst of all – to call God a liar. It's an offensive way to treat the Ruler of the universe. The alternative, according to John, is to enter heaven's court knowing that you're guilty, but with Jesus Christ as your attorney.

Another Bible passage gives the two options as these: 'Whoever believes in the Son has eternal life, but whoever rejects the Son will not see life, for God's wrath remains on them.'[42]

The stakes are high. This is not an ice-cream flavour issue. The options are binary. There isn't a middle option. Just like in our medical analogy, to endlessly delay treatment is to choose to die.

As we will see in a moment, Jesus famously made a similar argument concerning travel plans. Imagine you need to travel urgently from London to Edinburgh. You arrive at King's Cross station with a variety of options:

- Buy an expensive ticket and get on the train marked 'Edinburgh'.

- Reject the train company's signage as a fraud and get on the much cheaper train marked 'King's Lynn', sure that it must eventually reach Scotland.

- Be agnostic about whether to get on the Edinburgh train, and remain undecided on the platform as the doors close and it pulls out of the station.

If we don't decide, time decides for us.

We've made the choice seem a bit obvious and silly, but actually the train station dilemma represents a genuine quandary that thinking people face. At the spiritual railway interchange, if we can put it that way, there are lots of different options. Muslims urge us to get on one train, Buddhists another, atheists still another. The trains don't even *claim* to be headed for the same destination. The Hindu train is on a loop, promising the same stops over and over again in a cycle of reincarnation, until you attain a final state of oneness with the universe. The Buddhist train accelerates to escape velocity, catapulting you into Nirvana, a place of nothingness where all personality and relationships and meaning are dissolved. The three great monotheistic monorails – Judaism, Christianity and Islam – all warn of a fork in the track, leading to heaven / paradise or hell, though their descriptions of what these places are like differ hugely. Some atheists question whether there is a train at all, tending to nihilism and despair, but the majority look optimistically to a future where human society evolves to the point that it solves all of our problems, if only we would throw off the dangerous shackles of religion.

You have to evaluate whether a given religion or philosophy can actually *get you* to the destination promised. There are two issues here. First, is the train company a fraud? The religions of the world make such wildly divergent claims that they can't all be true.[43] Some people give up at this point, objecting that they just don't have time to look into every single religion. Fair enough. But Christianity should probably be top of your shortlist. To see why, make a list of the five most influential people in the history of the world. Now put an asterisk next to any on that list who have claimed to be the Creator and Saviour of the world.[44] That gives you just one name. It makes sense to start with Jesus.

Second, do you have a valid ticket? Have you satisfied the requirements of your chosen religion in terms of your moral performance or religious observances? There are many Muslims who are convinced of Islam but agnostic about their own place in paradise for this reason. There are Hindus who doubt their own karma.

As we've already noted, it's one of the unique features of Christianity that Jesus buys the ticket for you rather than asking you to scrape together the moral funds yourself.

So we grant that it's a tricky decision. You'd be forgiven for pausing for some time at the departures board. But our point stands. The one way you can be *certain* of not arriving *anywhere* is to remain undecided at the train station for the rest of your life.

Jesus described the decision not in terms of trains (which would have been somewhat anachronistic) but in terms of gates and roads:

> *Enter through the narrow gate. For wide is the gate and broad is the road that leads to destruction, and many enter through it. But small is the gate and narrow the road that leads to life, and only a few find it.*[45]

Jesus is clear that there are only two choices, and only two outcomes. And it's clear from his analogy (and from common sense) that when choosing a road, the popularity of the route and the comfort of the journey are ultimately irrelevant in comparison with the destination. If you need to go from London to Edinburgh, you would never even consider taking the M23 south towards Brighton, even if many of your friends are travelling that way and it's your absolute favourite road with the most pleasing camber you have ever experienced. The right choice might be unpopular. It might be difficult. But the wise person decides the route that leads to life.

To restate our earlier conclusions:

- The stakes are high. This is not an ice-cream flavour issue.

- The options are binary. There isn't a middle option.

- It's dangerous to remain agnostic.

Who's Playing Hide-and-Seek?

Pickles the dog has gone down in history as a national hero, having found the stolen Jules Rimet World Cup trophy while out for a walk with his owner David Corbett in March 1966.

Monika Lendl recently discovered WASP-189 b, an exoplanet 1.6 times the size of Jupiter with half the surface temperature of our sun, having conducted the search using the CHEOPS satellite.

Andrew was late for work because he had spent 40 minutes looking for his keys and then a further 20 minutes looking for his wallet before then trying to remember where he had parked his car the night before.

The world at every level is engaged in some sort of searching. Searching for stuff, searching for purpose, searching for answers, searching for the hero inside yourself, searching for meaning, searching for that special someone. We even tell ourselves that we are searching for God. He must be hiding somewhere, if he exists at all, and we are really doing our very utmost to find him. It might shock you, therefore, to hear the Bible's damning verdict on the human race: 'there is no one who seeks God'.[46]

The Bible insists that humans are far from being on the lookout for God. Ever since our first ancestors rejected their Creator, we have been on the run from him. Here is the account from its opening chapters:

Then the man and his wife heard the sound of the LORD God as he was walking in the garden in the cool of the day, and they hid from the LORD God among the trees of the garden. But the LORD God called to the man, 'Where are you?'

He answered, 'I heard you in the garden, and I was afraid because I was naked; so I hid.'[47]

The (almost) universal fear of being naked is more than a guilty conscience about missed visits to the gym and an overfamiliarity with Papa John's. It's bound up with a fear of being exposed, of being found out, of being seen for what we really are. The exception might be where there is innocence (as with a child) or intimacy (as with a sexual partner). But with God we are neither innocent nor intimate. So we hide.

Jesus put it like this:

This is the verdict: light has come into the world, but people loved darkness instead of light because their deeds were evil. Everyone who does evil hates the light, and will not come into the light for fear that their deeds will be exposed. But whoever lives by the truth comes into the light, so that it may be seen plainly that what they have done has been done in the sight of God.[48]

We are like spiritual cockroaches, moral photophobes who scuttle for cover, hunkering down in the shadows.

But how do we square that verdict with the apparently sincere religious quest of billions throughout history? In his book *Living with the Gods*, former director of the British Museum Neil MacGregor catalogues examples of shrines and sacred symbols, icons and inspired inscriptions, rituals and religious relics from all over the world. Doesn't this prove that we are spiritual seekers? No. The Bible views these very things as proof that we are hiding: 'They exchanged the truth about God for a lie, and worshipped and served created things rather than the Creator.'[49]

When an ancient civilisation makes little statues and calls them 'gods', or when a twenty-first-century theologian proposes a new way of updating orthodox doctrines to match the current zeitgeist, they are taking control of religion *in order to put distance* between themselves and the true and living God.[50] Their creativity is an act of concealment. Their professed truth-seeking is in fact truth-suppression.

If there is a cosmic game of hide-and-seek, we are the ones who are hiding. But the glorious news is that God is seeking. At the centre of the gospel is not a search *by* us, but a search *for* us. As an old hymn puts it,

> *I sought the Lord, and afterward I knew*
> *He moved my soul to seek him, seeking me.*
> *It was not I that found, O Saviour true,*
> *No, I was found of thee.*[51]

Luke, another of the gospel writers (we've focussed previously on John's writings) gives prominence to Jesus' mission statement: 'the Son of Man came to seek and to save the lost'.[52] The saying comes at the end of an encounter that is so beautifully characteristic of Jesus' dealings with unlikely people that we wanted to quote it in full:

> *Jesus entered Jericho and was passing through. A man was there by the name of Zacchaeus; he was a chief tax collector and was wealthy. He wanted to see [literally, 'he was seeking to see'] who Jesus was, but because he was short he could not see over the crowd. So he ran ahead and climbed a sycamore-fig tree to see him, since Jesus was coming that way.*

When Jesus reached the spot, he looked up and said to him, 'Zacchaeus, come down immediately. I must stay at your house today.' So he came down at once and welcomed him gladly.

All the people saw this and began to mutter, 'He has gone to be the guest of a sinner.'

But Zacchaeus stood up and said to the Lord, 'Look, Lord! Here and now I give half of my possessions to the poor, and if I have cheated anybody out of anything, I will pay back four times the amount.'

Jesus said to him, 'Today salvation has come to this house, because this man, too, is a son of Abraham. For the Son of Man came to seek and to save the lost.'[53]

The story begins with Zacchaeus seeking to see Jesus, but he is finally saved because Jesus had sought him.

It's a story of astonishing inclusivity. As a tax collector, Zacchaeus would have been ostracised and despised, a Jewish traitor on the payroll of the Roman occupying forces. At Jesus' initiative, he is welcomed as an insider, a 'son of Abraham'.

We know from Zacchaeus' own confession that he had cheated, swindled, deceived and extorted others in order to get ahead. He's not the likeliest religious convert ... except that he is! People like Zacchaeus have always loved Jesus. People who are conscious that they've messed up morally. People who know they've failed God and failed others. People who are surprised that God is interested in them, that he is out looking for them. Whereas the morally 'superior' resent him and sniff and scoff.

I (Andrew) remember years ago visiting a friend whose church was trying to help with the rehabilitation of offenders who had become Christians while in prison. We shared a car journey with a former inmate who told me, 'It's amazing what God is doing inside that prison. All sorts of people are getting converted. Some of them even worse than me!'

Contrast his humility and joy with the outrage of the Duchess of Buckingham, who wrote to her Christian friend the Countess of Huntingdon to decline an invitation to hear the eighteenth-century preacher George Whitefield:

Their doctrines are most repulsive and strongly tinctured with impertinence and disrespect towards their superiors in perpetually endeavouring to level all ranks, and do away with all distinction. It is monstrous to be told that you have a heart as sinful as the common wretches that crawl on the earth. This is highly offensive and insulting; and I cannot but wonder that your Ladyship should relish any sentiments so much at variance with high rank and good breeding.[54]

Luke observes the same polarised reactions throughout his gospel. Tax collectors and sinners gravitate to Jesus. The religious elite (the Pharisees) castigate him.

After this, Jesus went out and saw a tax collector by the name of Levi sitting at his tax booth. 'Follow me,' Jesus said to him, and Levi got up, left everything and followed him.

Then Levi held a great banquet for Jesus at his house, and a large crowd of tax collectors and others were eating with them. But the Pharisees and the teachers of the law who belonged to their sect complained to his disciples, 'Why do you eat and drink with tax collectors and sinners?'

Jesus answered them, 'It is not the healthy who need a doctor, but the sick. I have not come to call the righteous, but sinners to repentance.'[55]

We've explored Jesus' medical analogy already. If you know you have a life-threatening spiritual illness, then you're overjoyed to meet the doctor. If you think that you're fine, then you have little time for him yourself, and you scorn those hobbling into his waiting room on their religious crutches. Why would Jesus hang out at a dinner party with the morally diseased?

Some chapters later we meet the same two groups again:

All the people, even the tax collectors, when they heard Jesus' words, acknowledged that God's way was right, because they had been baptised by John. But the Pharisees and the experts in the law rejected God's purpose for themselves, because they had not been baptised by John.[56]

So the tax collectors were the ones who were baptised, and they welcomed Jesus. The Pharisees refused to be baptised, and they rejected Jesus. The key here is the meaning of the baptism – not merely a cultural rite of passage, as it has become for some today, but a 'baptism of repentance for the forgiveness of sins'.[57] Being plunged into the River Jordan symbolised the desire to be washed clean of moral filth. The Pharisees, who considered themselves whiter than white, didn't see the need to get even their toes wet.

Immediately after making this observation Luke tells us about another dinner party:

> When one of the Pharisees invited Jesus to have dinner with him, he went to the Pharisee's house and reclined at the table. A woman in that town who lived a sinful life learned that Jesus was eating at the Pharisee's house, so she came there with an alabaster jar of perfume. As she stood behind him at his feet weeping, she began to wet his feet with her tears. Then she wiped them with her hair, kissed them and poured perfume on them.

When the Pharisee who had invited him saw this, he said to himself, 'If this man were a prophet, he would know who is touching him and what kind of woman she is – that she is a sinner.'

Jesus answered him, 'Simon, I have something to tell you.'

'Tell me, teacher,' he said.

'Two people owed money to a certain money-lender. One owed him five hundred denarii, and the other fifty. Neither of them had the money to pay him back, so he forgave the debts of both. Now which of them will love him more?'

Simon replied, 'I suppose the one who had the bigger debt forgiven.'

'You have judged correctly,' Jesus said.

Then he turned towards the woman and said to Simon, 'Do you see this woman? I came into your house. You did not give me any water for my feet, but she wet my feet with her tears and wiped them with her hair. You did not give me a kiss, but this woman, from the time I entered, has not stopped kissing my feet. You did not put oil on my head, but she has poured

> *perfume on my feet. Therefore, I tell you, her many sins have been forgiven – as her great love has shown. But whoever has been forgiven little loves little.'*
>
> *Then Jesus said to her, 'Your sins are forgiven.'*
>
> *The other guests began to say among themselves, 'Who is this who even forgives sins?'*
>
> *Jesus said to the woman, 'Your faith has saved you; go in peace.'*[58]

Each of us is represented somewhere in this story. Some of you are agnostic, not about God's existence, but about whether he would accept you. Perhaps you're conscious of a shameful past. Perhaps you're trapped right now in a lifestyle that you know is wrong. And you doubt whether Jesus would give you the time of day. That's how this woman must have felt right up to the day she first met Jesus. But he cancelled her debts; he forgave her sins; he gave her a fresh start. And so she loved him – to such an extent that she now gatecrashes this posh soirée in order to drench Jesus with perfume and gratitude and tears.

Others of you instinctively side with Simon. You find her public display frankly embarrassing. Clearly Christianity is a magnet for the inadequate – not for someone as successful and well-rounded as you. You're not aware of any religious debts, and if you were, you'd pay them yourself. You don't want charity. You're self-made, self-sufficient, self-contained, self-righteous.

A few chapters further on we meet our now familiar actors yet again:

> Now the tax collectors and sinners were all gathering around to hear Jesus. But the Pharisees and the teachers of the law muttered, 'This man welcomes sinners and eats with them.'
>
> Then Jesus told them this parable…[59]

And Jesus goes on to tell three stories about things that get lost and a God who goes looking for them. In the first, God is likened to a shepherd on a rescue mission to save a lost sheep. In the second, he is like a woman who has lost a valuable coin and sweeps every corner of the house until she finds it. In the third, and most famous, he is a father who runs to welcome home a 'prodigal son' who had earlier disowned him.

Alongside the unifying lost–found theme, all three stories are marked by contagious joy on the part of the divine seeker:

> *And when he finds [the sheep], he joyfully puts it on his shoulders and goes home. Then he calls his friends and neighbours together and says, 'Rejoice with me; I have found my lost sheep.'*
>
> *And when she finds [the coin], she calls her friends and neighbours together and says, 'Rejoice with me; I have found my lost coin.'*
>
> *But the father said to his servants, 'Quick! Bring the best robe and put it on [the prodigal son]. Put a ring on his finger and sandals on his feet. Bring the fattened calf and kill it. Let's have a feast and celebrate. For this son of mine was dead and is alive again; he was lost and is found.' So they began to celebrate.*[60]

All three describe people changing their lives around: 'In the same way, I tell you, there is rejoicing in the presence of the angels of God over one sinner who repents.'[61] God finding someone and that person turning to him are two facets of the same reality.[62]

But there is a sting in the tale (sic). There is one character in the final story who is less than exuberant at the prodigal's return – and we're not talking about the calf with the elevated BMI! There is an older brother who…

> … *became angry and refused to go in. So his father went out and pleaded with him. But he answered his father, 'Look! All these years I've been slaving for you and never disobeyed your orders. Yet you never gave me even a young goat so I could celebrate with my friends. But when this son of yours who has squandered your property with prostitutes comes home, you kill the fattened calf for him!'*[63]

It's obvious that the older brother is intended to epitomise the attitude of the Pharisees. Their grumbling, you will remember, occasioned Jesus' lost–found trilogy in the first place. They think they've behaved impeccably and they resent God's kindness to the undeserving. But the irony is that they are the ones who end up out of sorts with God. In Jesus' parable, as with all of the real-life dinner parties Jesus attends, the supposed insider ends up on the outside, while the outsider is welcomed in.

We meet the Pharisee and the tax collector one last time:

To some who were confident of their own righteousness and looked down on everyone else, Jesus told this parable: 'Two men went up to the temple to pray, one a Pharisee and the other a tax collector. The Pharisee stood by himself and prayed: "God, I thank you that I am not like other people – robbers, evildoers, adulterers – or even like this tax collector. I fast twice a week and give a tenth of all I get."

'But the tax collector stood at a distance. He would not even look up to heaven, but beat his breast and said, "God, have mercy on me, a sinner."

'I tell you that this man, rather than the other, went home justified before God. For all those who exalt themselves will be humbled,

and those who humble themselves will be exalted.'[64]

The Pharisee saunters up to God, boasting in his own spiritual credentials. If the parable were set in the twenty-first century, you can be sure that he would be a carbon-neutral flexitarian, a campaigner for equal pay and racial justice, an all-round respectable guy. He even catalogues all sorts of bad things that he *didn't* do, in much the same way that family members often impress upon the vicar at funerals that the deceased 'never did anyone any harm' (a statement that is true of none of us). The Pharisee is nauseatingly smug, certain of his moral superiority.

The tax collector is starkly different. Instead of marching to the front, he cowers at the back. Instead of bragging about his merit, he throws himself on God's mercy. He alone, says Jesus, went home in the right with God.

To pull the threads together, we'd like to put to you three questions:

1. Do you insist that you are searching, or are you willing to admit you've been hiding?

2. Are you ready to repent / to be found? How you answer will likely depend on your response to the third question:

3. Are you on Team Pharisee or Team Tax Collector? That is to say, are you confident of your own righteousness, or are you a sinner seeking mercy?

We Write This to Make Our Joy Complete

We believe in Marxfreudanddarwin.
We believe everything is OK
as long as you don't hurt anyone,
to the best of your definition of hurt,
and to the best of your knowledge.
[...]
We believe that each man must find the truth
that is right for him.
Reality will adapt accordingly.
The universe will readjust. History will alter.
We believe that there is no absolute truth
excepting the truth that there is no absolute truth.

We believe in the rejection of creeds.[65]

These lines from the ironic poem by Steve Turner poke fun at the postmodern idea that we can choose our own reality. Sure, in the twenty-first century we have more self-determination than in any other age. We can choose our A levels, our career path, our Facebook friends, our hair colour, our wardrobe, our gender (?), our diet, our leisure activities, our reading material – for example, a fascinating book on agnosticism. But there remain external realities that we can't choose. We can't choose the past. We can't choose the laws of nature. We can't choose to add a single hour to our span of life.[66]

The Battle of Hastings took place between the English and the Normans in a field in the south-east of England in the year 1066. If you say that 'for you' it happened in 1266 between the Welsh and the Congolese, then you're just wrong. Granted, there might be subjective *interpretations* of history, but actual events won't bend to our whim.

Similarly, although it's common for people to brush off urgent spiritual questions with the protestation, 'I'm not the religious type,' you don't hear anyone claiming, 'I'm not the gravitational type.' I mean, you might not believe in gravity, but gravity believes in you. (In fact it's very attracted to you!) Jumping off a tall building thinking you can fly is not recommended.

If you have any sense, you base subjective decisions on objective realities. It might surprise you to learn that the Bible agrees. Nowhere is 'faith' defined as the thing required to bridge the gap that rationality won't close. Indeed, we are never invited to *believe* anything without being given a reason. In a letter to a first-century church in Corinth, the apostle Paul was very candid: 'if Christ has not been raised, our preaching is useless and so is your faith. More than that, we are then found to be false witnesses about God...'[67]

Faith in Christ only stands if built on the foundation of a resurrection that actually happened. That's why, for the majority of this book, we've tried to confront you with objective arguments rather than opinions, with facts rather than warm fuzzies.

But that's not to say that warm fuzzies are irrelevant. In the opening pages of this book, we noted that many people keep Jesus at arm's length for fear that he might suck the fun out of the room. Now, in this final chapter, we want to testify to the opposite. He is the one who enables us to live life to the full.

One of the strange things you'll notice as you encounter real Christians is that some of those who have suffered the most are agnostic the least. You'd expect their trials would lead them to doubt God's goodness, but the opposite is true. Instead of abandoning their faith, they cling to their Saviour all the more.

Atheism, as an alternative, is impotent. There's no comfort in chance molecular collisions. A materialistic universe is silent in the face of suffering. Viewed through the lens of the Darwinistic mechanism alone, the weeding out of the weakest in society at the hands of the strong is pure progress.

But it's not a mere preference for Christian philosophy that keeps these believers going. It's a personal relationship with a God who loves them, understands them, cares deeply for them and is able to help them. They know this *objectively* – Jesus really went to the cross to pay their ransom and rose from the dead to give them a sure future hope. But they also know it *subjectively*, in their experience.

A friend of ours, Alvis, who works in a former communist country, became a church minister some time before coming to a personal faith in Christ. Church attendance had been severely restricted under the Soviets, but after the fall of the Iron Curtain in 1989, people rushed to fill the pews. This created a demand for clerics, and the authorities were ready to hand out the keys of ancient churches to anyone who could provide basic credentials. Thus Alvis saw a promising career opportunity.

Each Saturday night he would scribble down a sermon that he didn't really believe in, before sitting down to enjoy a cigar. Until there came a week when he was due to preach on the feeding of the 5000. He couldn't for the life of him work out how Jesus had done it! Alvis sweated over his preparation, struggling to ascertain how Jesus could possibly have fed so many mouths with so little food – and he smoked a great many cigars that night! Finally, he found relief in a sceptical tome that suggested Jesus' personality was so powerful that people *felt* full in his presence, even though their stomachs were empty. Alvis was extremely pleased with himself and looked forward to sharing his clever findings with his parishioners the following day.

At the door, after church, an older lady thanked him for his message, though she was a bit deaf and seemed not to have followed the argument. The sun was at her face, and she smiled, as if transported back in her memory for an instant. Then she said, softly, 'God was so kind to us in the Gulag.'

Alvis felt a sudden and intense shame. Here he was, awaiting congratulations for having (he thought) explained away God's power, shaking hands with a woman who had known its reality amid the untold horrors of a communist labour camp. His empty cynicism was confronted by her inexpressible and glorious joy.

It was a turning point in his own spiritual journey. Now he too is a real Christian (and a real Christian minister!). He cares passionately about the objective basis of the faith, and he would be the first to impress upon an agnostic the extensive evidence for Jesus' bread-multiplying miracle. Yet he also knows Jesus subjectively.

He's trusted him for many years. A sparkle comes into his own eyes now when he speaks of Jesus' kindness and faithfulness to him.

Let's finish by revisiting these profound words of the apostle John:

> That which was from the beginning, which we have heard, which we have seen with our eyes, which we have looked at and our hands have touched – this we proclaim concerning the Word of life. The life appeared; we have seen it and testify to it, and we proclaim to you the eternal life, which was with the Father and has appeared to us. We proclaim to you what we have seen and heard, so that you also may have fellowship with us. And our fellowship is with the Father and with his Son, Jesus Christ. We write this to make our joy complete.[68]

The Agnostic Diagnostic (Revisited)

1 Strongly agree	2 Agree	3 Neither agree nor disagree	4 Disagree	5 Strongly disagree
I've started on a journey that is already beginning to change my life.	I've started on a journey that could change my life.	I'm still on the fence, but the splinters are beginning to dig into my backside.	Reading this book wasted a couple of hours I will never get back; hopefully it can be recycled to make eco-friendly toilet paper.	I have already set fire to the corner of this book, and the warm glow I now experience from its pages is the first tangible benefit it has brought me.

☐ Jesus isn't just a fairy tale; the evidence for his life, death and resurrection is compelling.

☐ Jesus doesn't want to wreck my life, but to bring me joy through a relationship with the God who made me.

☐ There's no such thing as neutrality; there's a chance I could reject what I know to be true because I'm afraid of its implications.

☐ I need forgiveness from God, and the only place it can be found is in the death of Jesus.

☐ There's nothing more important than for me to get to the bottom of this.

☐ I'm not 100% sure I want to be an agnostic.

References

In God We Doubt?

1   A phrase coined by Richard Dawkins, perhaps Britain's most vocal atheist.

2   https://en.wikipedia.org/wiki/List_of_agnostics, accessed August 2019.

3   John Humphrys, *In God We Doubt: Confessions of a Failed Atheist* (London: Hodder and Stoughton, 2008), pp. 36–37.

4   Marcus Brigstocke, *God Collar* (London: Corgi, 2012), pp. 13–14.

What Kind of Agnostic Are You Anyway?

5   Confusingly, agnosticism is not the opposite of Gnosticism, a strange religious movement in the second century whose adherents claimed special spiritual insight.

6   For those eager to learn, Jon offers the following definitions: a yorker is a fast ball aimed at the batsman's feet; a googly is a slow spinning delivery that the batsman thinks is going to bounce and spin one way, but actually spins the other way; Geoffrey Boycott was a famous English batsman who batted for hours without scoring any runs…

7   A sickly sweet, non-alcoholic, sparkling grape juice sold in the UK.

Meet the Truth

8   https://whitecube.com/exhibitions/exhibition/the_real_three_propositions_bermondsey_2019.

9   www.alankoppel.com/exhibitions/peter-dreher-day-by-day-good-day.

10   1 John 1:1–3.

11   J. Jeremias, 'The rediscovery of Bethesda: John 5:2', New Testament Archaeology Monographs No. 1 (1966).

12   Counterintuitively, during crucifixion it is breathing *out* that requires effort: with the

weight of the body hanging from the arms, the ribcage is raised, putting the victim 'into an almost perpetual state of inhalation' (Alok Jha, 'How did crucifixion kill?' *The Guardian*, 8 April 2004).

13 John 19:34.

14 For example, Jesus had challenged his opponents, 'Destroy this temple, and I will raise it again in three days', speaking enigmatically of his own body (John 2:19, cf. verse 22), and later told his disciples that 'I have authority to lay [my life] down and authority to take it up again' (John 10:18).

15 In fact, Thomas is the patron saint of surveyors, builders, and architects, but that didn't seem as immediately relevant.

Blind Men Are Sometimes the Best Eyewitnesses!

16 Thanks to our friend Alistair Tresidder for pointing us to this remarkable story.

17 'Archaeologists identify traces of 'miracle' pool', http://www.nbcnews.com/id/6750670#.XoRjzS3MzyU, accessed 2 April 2020.

18 Exodus 20:8–9.

19 John 7:27. The controversy about Jesus' origins is one of the big themes of John's Gospel. On hearing that Jesus is from Nazareth, Nathanael exclaims, 'Nazareth! Can anything good come from there?' (1:46).

20 Translation: 'All the best lawyers express themselves in Latin.'

The Curious Case of Mr P

21 American readers will perhaps know this children's game by the name 'Telephone'.

22 This section engaging with Dan Brown is reproduced, with permission of the publisher, from Andrew Sach and Tim Hiorns, *Dig Deeper into the Gospels* (Nottingham: IVP, 2015).

23 Irenaeus of Lyon, *Against Heresies*, 3.11.8.

24 Gospel of Thomas, verse 114.

25 See Matthew 27:3–9.

26 For a more thorough exploration of this particular issue, we recommend James Bejon's article 'Judas's demise in Matthew 27 and Acts 1. Do they contradict?'

https://www.thegospelcoalition.org/
article/judas-demise-matthew-1-acts-1.

27 Peter J. Williams, *Can We Trust the Gospels?*
(Wheaton, IL: Crossway, 2018).

Even More Syllogisms (for the Enthusiast)

28 There are some excellent videos explaining
this further at https://www.reasonablefaith.
org/kalam/.

29 For example, anti-Semitism in Nazi
Germany, or the widely accepted practice
in ancient Greece and Rome of abandoning
unwanted infants, particularly girls, to die.

30 Genesis 1:27; Psalm 98:9.

31 John Lennox, *God's Undertaker: Has Science
Buried God?* (Oxford: Lion Hudson, 2009).

32 The historian Tom Holland cites many such
instances in *Dominion: The Making of the
Western Mind* (London: Little, Brown, 2019).

33 Revelation 21:4.

34 'Jesus of the Scars' by Edward Shillito
(1872–1948).

35 See Luke 13:1–9. The writer C. S. Lewis famously said of God that pain was 'His megaphone to rouse a deaf world', *The Problem of Pain* (New York: HarperOne, 2001), p. 91.

It's Dangerous to Remain Agnostic

36 1 John 1:5.

37 1 John 1: 6–7.

38 John 7:17.

39 1 John 1:8–9.

40 A clear conscience is not as unattainable as Sir Humphrey Appleby implies (a reference fans of the classic TV series *Yes, Prime Minister* will appreciate – see https://youtu.be/jNKjShmHw7s).

41 1 John 1:10 – 2:2.

42 John 3:36.

43 For example, the Qur'an insists that Jesus was not crucified (look up surah 4:157 on quran.com), whereas the Bible insists he was. They cannot both be correct.

44 This idea is adapted from Tim Keller, *Making Sense of God: An Invitation to the Sceptical* (London: Hodder and Stoughton, 2018). The advantage of this intersection-on-the-Venn-diagram approach is that it eliminates the many lunatics who have claimed to be God but made no impact whatsoever on world history.

45 Matthew 7:13–14.

Who's Playing Hide-and-Seek?

46 Romans 3:11.

47 Genesis 3:8–10.

48 John 3:19–21.

49 Romans 1:25.

50 It's striking how often the Bible describes God as the 'living God', making a distinction with the lifeless idols that we make up ourselves. See Deuteronomy 5:26; Joshua 3:10; 1 Samuel 17:26, 36; 2 Kings 19:4, 16; Psalm 42:2; 84:2; Isaiah 37:4, 17; Jeremiah 10:10; 23:36; Daniel 6:20, 26; Hosea 1:10; Matthew 16:16; 26:63; Acts

14:15; Romans 9:26; 2 Corinthians 3:3; 6:16; 1 Timothy 3:15; 4:10; Hebrews 3:12; 9:14; 10:31; 12:22; Revelation 7:2.

51 Hymn by Jean Ingelow (1878).

52 Luke 19:10.

53 Luke 19:1–10.

54 John Pollock, *George Whitefield and the Great Awakening* (London: Hodder and Stoughton, 1972), p. 95.

55 Luke 5:27–32 (our italics).

56 Luke 7:29–30 (our italics).

57 Luke 3:3.

58 Luke 7:36–50 (our italics).

59 Luke 15:1–3 (our italics).

60 Luke 15:5–6, 9, 22–24.

61 Luke 15:10.

62 We would have said 'two sides of the same coin', but we thought that might confuse matters!

63 Luke 15:28–30.

64   Luke 18:9–14 (our italics).

We Write This to Make Our Joy Complete

65   Steve Turner, *Up to Date: Poems 1968–1982* (London: Hodder and Stoughton, 1982). Used with the author's permission.

66   As Jesus observed in Matthew 6:27.

67   1 Corinthians 15:14–15.

68   1 John 1:1–4.